Christmas
South of the Border
—∼—

Featuring The Red Hot Jalapeños
With Special Guest, The Cactus Brothers
Add heat to your holiday with these Sala-flavored arrangements
+
"X"
"XXX"
"XXXXX"
"GOD JUL"
"BUON AN"
"FELIZ NATAL"
"JOYEUX NOEL"
"VESELE VANOCE"
"MELE KALIKIMAKA"
"NODLAG SONA DHUIT"
"BLWYDDYN NEWYDD DDA"
""""""BOAS FESTAS""""""
"FELIZ NAVIDAD"
"MERRY CHRISTMAS"
"KALA CHRISTOUGENA"
"VROLIJK KERSTFEEST"
"FROHLICHE WEIHNACHTEN"
"BUON NATALE-GODT NYTAR"
"HUAN YING SHENG TAN CHIEH"

~ Special thanks to Jim Silvers at CMH records ~

Cover Art – J.J. Abbott
Cover Layout – Shawn Brown
Production – Ron Middlebrook
Guitar Transcribing & Notation – Steve Barden

ISBN 1-57424-132-X
SAN 683-8022

Table of Contents

Jingle Bells

Centerstream Publishing - P. O. Box 17878 – Anaheim Hills, CA 92817

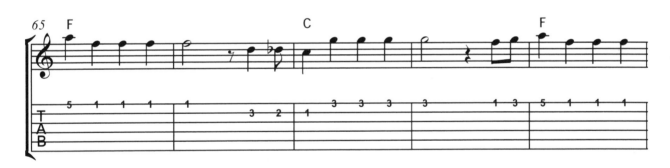

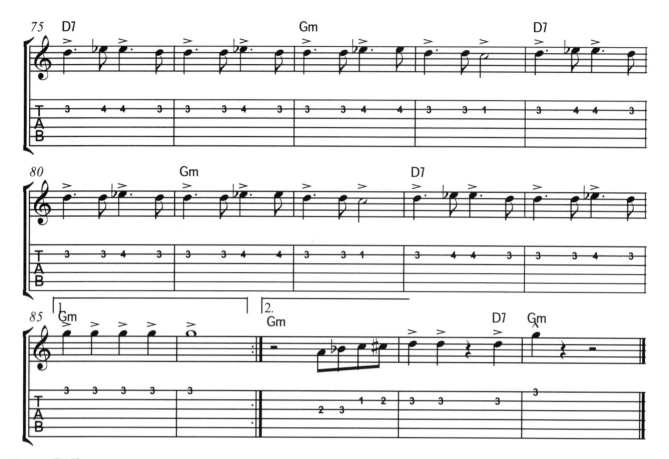

Jingle Bells

Dashing thru the snow
In a one horse open sleigh,
O'er the fields we go,
Laughing all the way;
Bells on bobtail ring,
Making spirits bright,
What fun it is to ride and sing
A sleighing song tonight!

Refrain:
Jingle bells, jingle bells!
Jingle all the way!
Oh what fun it is to ride
In a one horse open sleigh.

2.
A day or two ago,
I thought I'd take a ride,
And soon Miss Fanny Bright
Was seated by my side;
The horse was lean and lank;
Misfortune seemed his lot;
He got into a drifted bank,
And we, we got upsot. *Refrain:*

3.
A day or two ago,
The story I must tell
I went out on the snow
And on my back I fell;
A gent was riding by
In a one horse open sleigh,
He laughed as there I sprawling lie,
But quickly drove away. *Refrain:*

Cascabel

Ha llegado Navidad
La familia a le greestá
Esperando la Noche buena
En la paz del santo hogar.

Ha llegado Navidad
La familia a le greestá
Esperando la Noche Buena
En la paz del santo hogar.

Cascabel, Cascabel
Lindo Cascabel
Con sus notas de algría
Anuncia a Noel.

Cascabel, Cascabel
Lindo Cascabel
Con sus notas de algría
Anuncia a Noel.

Hark! The Herald Angels Sing

Centerstream Publishing - P. O. Box 17878 – Anaheim Hills, CA 92817

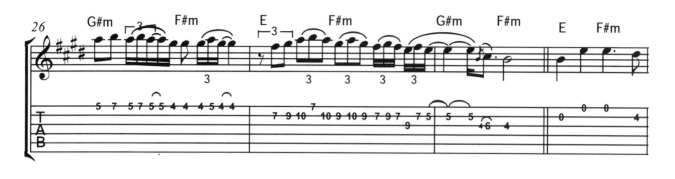

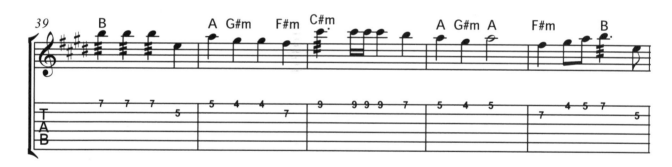

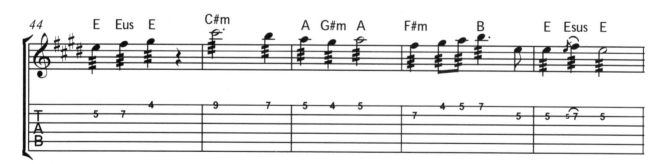

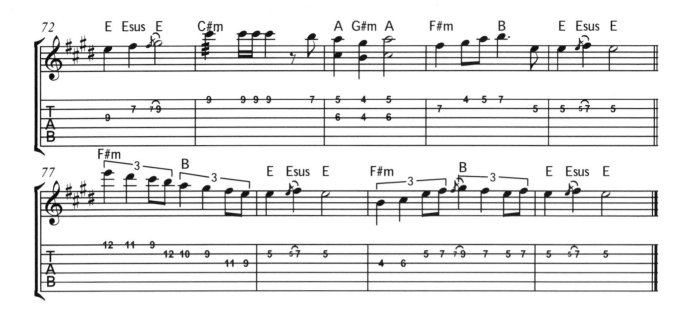

Hark the Herald Angels Sing

Hark! the herald angels sing.
"Glory to the new born King!
Peace on earth, and mercy mild;
God and sinners reconciled!"
Joyful, all ye nations rise,
Join the triumph of the skies;
With th'angelic hosts proclaim,
"Christ is born in Bethlehem!"

Refrain:
Hark! The herald angels sing,
"Glory to the new born King!"

2.
Christ, by highest heav'n adored;
Christ, the everlasting Lord;
Late in time behold Him come,
Offspring of the Virgin's womb.
Veiled in flesh the Godhead see;
Hail th' Incarnate Deity,
Pleased as man with man to dwell;
Jesus, our Emmanuel: *Refrain:*

3.
Hail, the heav'n-born Prince of Peace!
Hail, the Son of Righteousness!
Light and life to all He brings,
Ris'n with healing in His wings:
Mild He lays His glory by,
Born that man no more may die,
Born to raise the sons of earth,
Born to give them second birth: *Refrain:*

Escucha los Arcangeles Cantar

Al mortal, paz en la tierra;
En los cielos, Gloria a Dios.
Al mortal, paz en la tierra,
Canta la cleste voz.

Con los cielos alabemos;
Al eterno Rey cantemos.
A Jesús, a nuestro bien,
Con el coro de Belén,
Canta la celeste voz:
En los cielos
Gloria a Dios.

Escuchad el Son Triunfal

Escuchad el son triufal de la hueste celestial;
Paz y Buena voluntad; salvación Dios os dará.
Cante hoy toda nación la angelical canción;
Estas nuevas todos den; Nació Cristo en Belén.

¡Salve, Príncipe de Paz¡ Redención traído has,
luz y vida con virtud, en tus alas la salud.
De tu trono has bajado y la muerte conquistado
Para dar al ser mortal nacimiento celestial.

10

We Three Kings of Orient Are

Centerstream Publishing - P. O. Box 17878 – Anaheim Hills, CA 92817

13

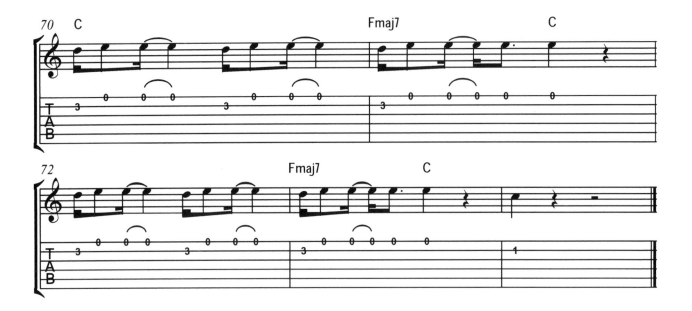

We Three Kings of Orient Are

We three kings of Orient are;
Bearing gifts we traverse afar
Field and fountain, moor and mountain,
Following yonder star:

Refrain:
O star of wonder, star of night,
Star with royal beauty bright,
Westward leading, still proceeding,
Guide us to thy perfect light.

2. (Melchior)
Born a king on Bethlehem plain,
Gold I bring to crown Him again –
King forever, ceasing never,
Over us all to reign: *Refrain:*

3. (Gaspar)
Frankincense to offer have I;
Incense owns a Deity nigh:
Prayer and praising, all men raising,
Worship Him, God most high: *Refrain:*

4. (Balthazar)
Myrrh is mine; its bitter perfume
Breathes a life of gathering gloom;
Sorrowing, sighing, bleeding, dying,
Sealed in the stone-cold tomb: *Refrain:*

5. (All)
Glorious now, behold Him arise,
King, and God, and Sacrifice!
Heaven sings "Alleluia!"
"Alleluia!" the earth replies: *Refrain:*

Los Reyes de Oriente

Los magos que llegaron
A Belén
Anunciando la llegada
Del Mesías,
A Jesús con alegría
Le cantamos hoy también.

De tierra lejana
Venimos a verte
Nos sirve de guía la Estrella de
Oriente.
¡Oh! Brillante estrella
que anuncia la aurora!
No me falte nunca
Tu luz bienechora.

Venid pastorcillos,
Venid a adorar
Al Rey de los Cielos
Que ha nacido ya.
**¡Gloria en las Alturas
al hijo de Dios!
¡Gloria en las Alturas
y en la tierra amor!**

14

We Wish You a Merry Christmas

Centerstream Publishing - P. O. Box 17878 – Anaheim Hills, CA 92817

We Wish You A Merry Christmas

We wish you a Merry Christmas,
We wish you a Merry Christmas,
We wish you a Merry Christmas,
And a happy New Year!

Refrain:
Glad tidings we bring
To you and your kin;
Glad tidings for Christmas
And a happy New Year!

2.
Please bring us some figgy pudding,
Please bring us some figgy pudding,
Please bring us some figgy pudding,
Please bring it right here! *Refrain:*

3.
We won't go until we get some,
We won't go until we get some,
We won't go until we get some,
Please bring it right here! *Refrain:*

4.
We wish you a Merry Christmas,
We wish you a Merry Christmas,
We wish you a Merry Christmas,
And a happy New Year! *Refrain:*

Feliz Navidad

Feliz Navidad.
Feliz Navidad.
Feliz Navidad, próspero año y felicidad.
Feliz Navidad.
Feliz Navidad.
Feliz Navidad, próspero año y felicidad.

I wanna wish you a merry Christmas.
I wanna wish you a merry Christmas.
I wanna wish you a merry Christmas
From the bottom of my heart.

I wanna wish you a merry Christmas.
I wanna wish you a merry Christmas.
I wanna wish you a merry Christmas
From the bottom of my heart.

Feliz Navidad.
Feliz Navidad.
Feliz Navidad, próspero año y felicidad.
Feliz Navidad.
Feliz Navidad.
Feliz Navidad, própero año y felicidad.

I wanna wish you a merry Christmas.
I wanna wish you a merry Christmas.
I wanna wish you a merry Christmas
From the bottom of my heart.
I wanna wish you a merry Christmas.
I wanna wish you a merry Christmas
I wanna wish you a merry Christmas
From the bottom of my heart.

Feliz Navidad.
Feliz Navidad.
Feliz Navidad próspero año y felicidad.
Feliz Navidad.
Feliz Navidad
Feliz Navidad, próspero año y felicidad.

Deck the Halls

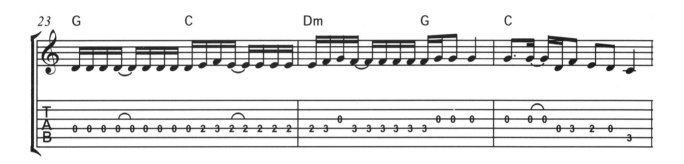

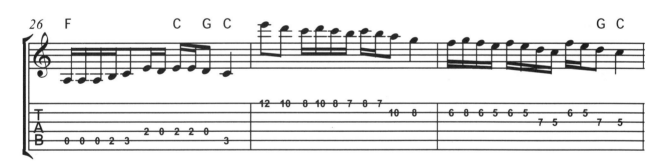

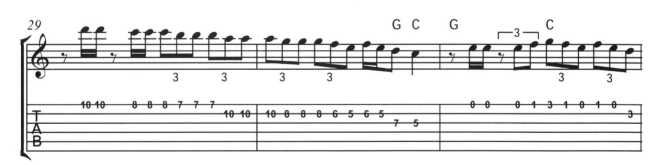

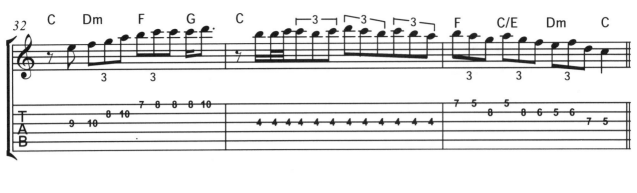

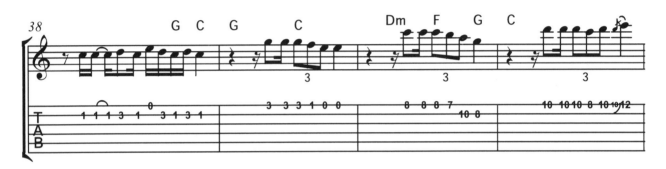

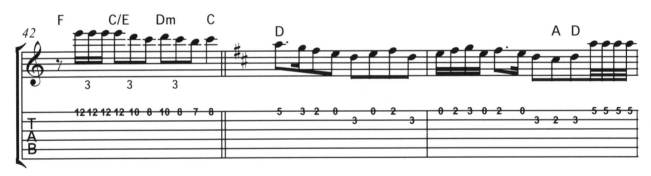

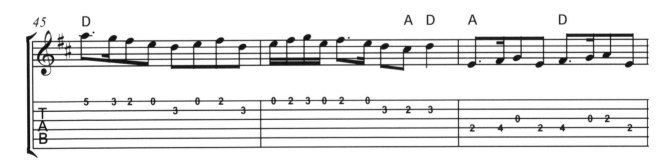

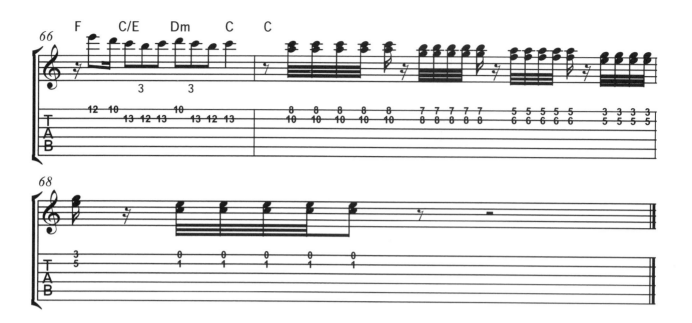

Deck the Halls

Deck the halls with boughs of holly,
Fa la la la la, la la la la;
'Tis the season to be jolly,
Fa la la la la, la la la la.
Don we now our gay apparel,
Fa la la, la la la, la la la;
Troll the ancient Yuletide carol,
Fa la la la la, la la la la.

2.

See the blazing yule before us,
Fa la la la la, la la la la;
Strike the harp and join the chorus,
Fa la la la la, la la la la.
Follow me in merry measure,
Fa la la, la la la, la la la
While I tell of Yuletide treasure,
Fa la la la la, la la la la.

3.

Fast away the old year passes,
Fa la la la la, la la la la;
Hail the New Year, lads and lasses,
Fa la la la la, la la la la,
Sing we joyous, all together,
Fa la la, la la la, la la la;
Heedless of the wind and weather,
Fa la la la la, la la la la.

What Child Is This

Centerstream Publishing - P. O. Box 17878 – Anaheim Hills, CA 92817

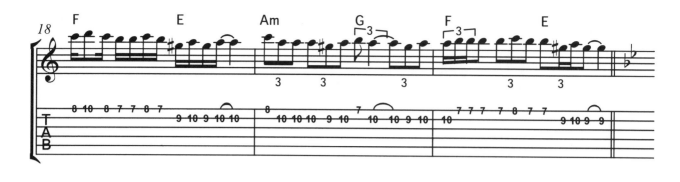

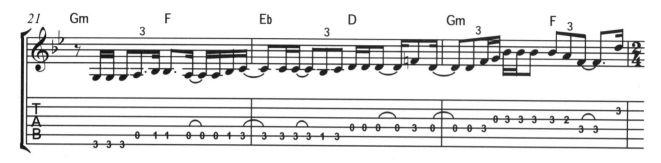

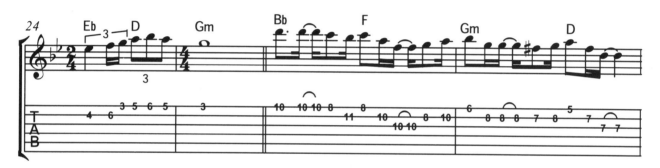

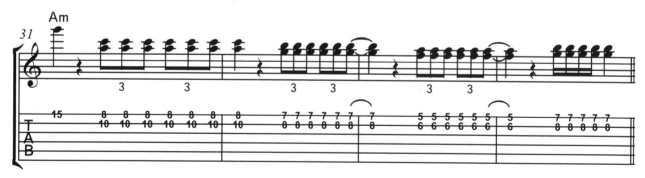

24

What Child Is This?

What Child is this, who, laid to rest,
On Mary's lap is sleeping?
Whom angels greet with anthems sweet,
While shepherds watch are keeping?

Refrain:
This, this is Christ the King,
Whom shepherds guard and angels sing:
Haste, haste to bring Him laud,
The Babe, the Son of Mary.

2.
Why lies He in such mean estate
Where ox and ass are feeding?
Good Christian, fear: for sinners here
The silent Word is pleading. *Refrain:*

3.
So bring Him incense, gold, and myrrh,
Come, peasant, King to own Him;
The King of Kings salvation brings,
Let loving hearts enthrone Him: *Refrain:*

¿Qué Niño es Éste?

¿Qué niño es éste que al dormir
en brazos de María, pastores velan,
ángeles le cantan melodías?
Él es el Cristo, el rey.
Pastores, ángeles cantan,
«Venid, venid a él, al hijo de María.»

¿Por qué en humilde establo así,
el niño es hoy nacido?
Por todoinjusto pecador
Su amor ha florecido.
Él es el Cristo, el rey.
Pastores, ángeles cantan,
«Venid, venid a él, al hijo de María.»

Traed ofrendas en su honor
El rey como el labriego,
Al rey de reyes, Salvador,
Un trono levantemos.
Él es el Cristo, el rey.
Pastores, ángeles cantan,
«Venid, venid a él, al hijo de María.»

Dime Niño de Quién Eres

Dime niño ¿ de quién eres
Todo vestido de blanco?
Soy de la Virgen María y del Espiritu Santo
Soy de la Virgen María y del Espiritu Santo

Soy amor en el pesebre y sufrimiento en la cruz.
Soy amor en el pesebre y sufrimiento en la cruz.
Resuenen con alegría los cánticos de mi tierra
Y viva el Niño de Dios que ha nacido en Noche Buena.
Resuenen con alegría los cánticos de mi tierra
Y viva el Niño de Dios que ha nacido en Noche Buena.

La Noche Buena se viene, tu ru ru la
La Noche Buena se va.
Y nosotros nos iremos, tu ru ru
Y no volveremos más.

Soy amor en el pesebre y sufrimiento el la cruz
Soy amor en el pesebre y sufrimiento el la cruz.

Qué Hermoso Niño

Qué hermoso Niño el que duerme allá
Que admira la Virgen María
A quien le cantan los ángeles
De amor y de prosperidad.

Celebremos llegó el rey
Con cantos de salvación y fe
Elevemos al niño Dios
El hijo de María.

What child is this who laid to rest
On Mary's lap is sleeping
Whom angels greet with anthems sweet
While shepherds watch are keeping

This, this is Christ the king
Whom shepherds guard and angels sing
Haste, haste to bring him laud
The babe, the Son of Mary.

Elevemos al niño Dios
El hijo de María.

26

God Rest Ye Merry Gentlemen

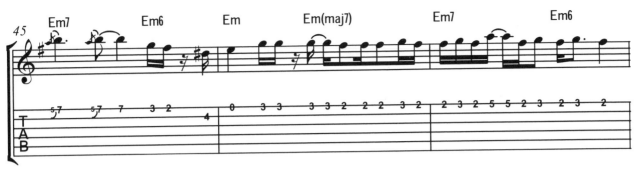

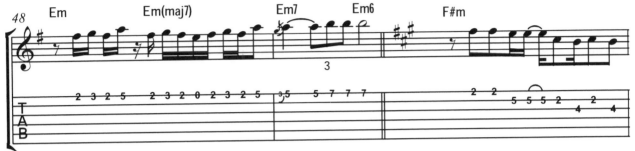

29

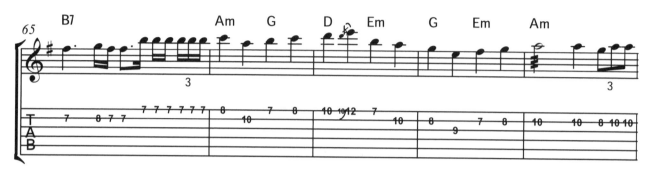

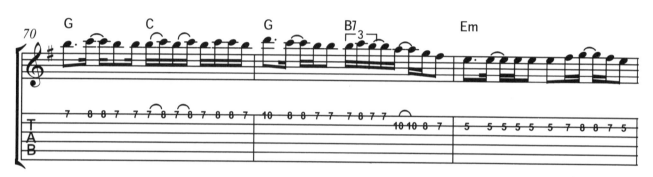

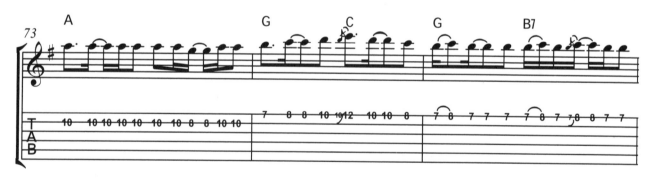

God Rest Ye Merry, Gentlemen

God rest ye merry, gentlemen,
Let nothing you dismay;
Remember Christ, our Saviour,
Was born on Christmas day,
To save us all from Satan's power
When we were gone astray:

Refrain:
O tidings of comfort and joy, comfort and joy;
O tidings of comfort and joy.

2.
In Bethlehem in Jewry
This blessed Babe was born,
And laid within a manger
Upon this blessed morn;
The which His mother, Mary,
Did nothing take in scorn: *Refrain:*

3.
From God, our heav'nly Father
A blessed angel came,
And unto certain shepherds
Brought tidings of the same,
How that in Bethlehem was born
The Son of God by name; *Refrain:*

4.
"Fear not," then aid the angel,
"Let nothing you affright,
This day is born a Saviour,
Of virtue, pow'r and might;
So frequently to vanquish all
The friends of Satan quite." *Refrain:*

30

Joy to the World

Centerstream Publishing - P. O. Box 17878 – Anaheim Hills, CA 92817

34

Joy To The World

Joy to the world! The Lord is come!
Let earth receive her King;
Let every heart prepare Him room,
And heav'n and nature sing; and heav'n and nature sing;
And heav'n, and heav'n and nature sing.

2.
Joy to the world! The Saviour reigns!
Let men their songs employ;
While fields and floods, rocks, hills and plains
Repeat the sounding joy, repeat the sounding joy;
Repeat, repeat the sounding joy.

3.
No more let sin and sorrow grow,
Nor thorns infest the ground;
He comes to make His blessings flow
Far as the curse is found, far as the curse is found,
Far as the curse is found.

4.
He rules the world with truth and grace,
And makes the nations prove
The glories of His righteousness,
And wonders of His love, and wonders of His love,
And wonders, wonders of His love.

¡Regocijad! Jesús Nació

¡Regocijad! Jesús nació, del mundo Salvador;
y cada corazón tornada recibir al Rey,
a recibir al Rey. Venid a recibir al Rey.

¡Regocijad! El reinará; cantemos en union;
y en la tierra y en el mar loor resonará.
Loor resonará, y gran loor resonará.

Ya lamaldad vencida es; la tierra paz tendrá.
La bendición del Salvador quitó la maldición,
Quitó la maldición; Jesús quitó la maldición.

¡Gloria a Dios cantemos hoy! Señor de Israel,
la libertad tú le darás y tú serás su Dios,
y tú serás su Dios,, Señor, y tú serás su Dios.

36

O Come All Ye Faithful

Centerstream Publishing - P. O. Box 17878 – Anaheim Hills, CA 92817

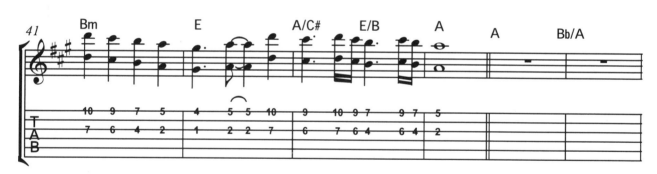

O Come, All Ye Faithful

O come, all ye faithful, joyful and triumphant,
O come ye, O come ye to Bethlehem!
Come and behold Him, born the King of Angels;

Refrain:
O come, let us adore Him,
O come, let us adore Him;
O come, let us adore Him,
Christ the Lord.

2.
Sing, choirs of angels, sing in exultation,
O sing, all ye citizens of heaven above!
Glory to God in the highest: *Refrain:*

3.
Yea, Lord, we greet Thee, born this happy morning,
Jesus, to Thee be all glory giv'n;
Word of the Father now in flesh appearing: *Refrain:*

Adeste Fideles

Venid, venid fideles ha nacido el niño Jesús,
Nuestro Salvador, venid a Belén.

El Rey del Cielo ha venido almundo.
Venid a contemplarle, venid y adoradle,
Venid y adoradle, esnuestro Señor.

Silent Night

Centerstream Publishing - P. O. Box 17878 – Anaheim Hills, CA 92817

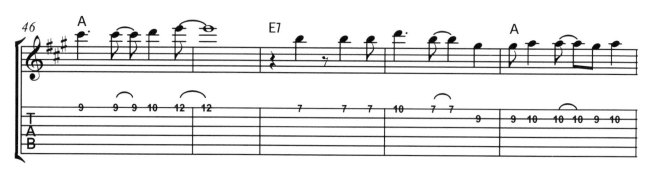

Silent Night

Silent night, holy night!
All is calm, all is bright
'Round yon Virgin Mother and Child
Holy Infant, so tender and mild,
Sleep in heavenly peace!
Sleep in heavenly peace!

2.
Silent night, holy night!
Shepherds quake at the sight.
Glories stream from heaven afar,
Heav'nly hosts sing "Alleluia!"
Christ the Saviour is born!
Christ the Saviour is born!

3.
Silent night, holy night!
Wondrous star, lend thy light!
With the angels let us sing
Alleluia to our Kind!
Christ the Saviour is here,
Jesus the Saviour is here!

4.
Silent night, holy night!
Son of God, love's pure light,
Radiant beams from Thy holy face,
With the dawn of redeeming grace,
Jesus, Lord, at Thy birth,
Jesus, Lord, at Thy birth!

Noche de Paz

Noche de paz, noche de amor,
Todo duerme en derredor.
Entre sus astros que esparcen su luz
Bella anunciando al niñito Jesús.
Brilla la estrella de paz,
Brilla la estrella de paz.

Noche de paz, noche de amor,
Todo duerme en derredor.
Sólo velan en la oscuridad
Los pastores que en el campo están
Y la estrella de Belén,
Y la estrella de Belén.

Noche de paz, noche de amor,
Todo duerme en derredor.
Sobre el santo niño Jesús
Una estrella esparce su luz,
Brilla sobre el Rey,
Brilla sobre el Rey.

Noche de paz, noche de amor,
Todo duerme en derredor;
Fieles velando allí en Belén
Los pastores, la madre también,
Y la estrella de paz,
Y la estrella de paz.